Sensual Lingerie

· THE · ART · OF ·
SILKEN SEDUCTION

Sensual Lingerie

· THE · ART · OF ·
SILKEN SEDUCTION

Text
Brad Stephen

Photography
Peter Barry, Peter Pugh-Cook, John Kelly
Black and white photographs copyright ©
The Hulton Deutsch Collection

Design
Stonecastle Graphics Ltd.

CLB 2617
© 1990 Colour Library Books Ltd., Godalming, Surrey, England.
This 1990 edition published by Crescent Books,
distributed by Outlet Book Company, Inc.,
a Random House Company,
225 Park Avenue South, New York, New York 10003.
Printed and bound in Singapore.
ISBN 0 517 05651 8
8 7 6 5 4 3 2 1

Colour is important. It has tremendous influence on everyone who can see. It has strong sexual connotations. It can please or disgust. In the animal kingdom we see daily evidence of how specially developed colour is used to attract a mate, or examples of a warning coloration (generally a vivid combination of black, white, red, or yellow) used to indicate that an insect is inedible or dangerous to a predator.

In past centuries and in most vertebrates it is the male who displays; who uses colour to impress and attract the female. In our present century, though there has been a definite move towards equality of the sexes in humans, it is the female who sets the pace in using colour to advantage.

We here look at colour in one particular context, and hear what poets and others have had to say on the subject.

Perfection in Pink

Pink is the new-born babe, the freshness of youth, the girl-child. Pink are the cheeks of the blushing milkmaid, the dawdling schoolgirl, the ingenue actress, the dowager duchess. In the pink of condition, in the best of health. 'Hoping this finds you in the pink, as it leaves me at present', wrote countless downstairs maids to the second footmen who had gone to be soldiers.

Thrift or Sea-Pinks may have had no use in physic, but were nonetheless cultivated in the 16th century 'for their beautie and pleasure in gardens'. The local names are almost as alluring as the colour: Cliff Rose, Cushion Pink, Lady's Pincushion, Midsummer Fairmaid, Rock Rose, or in the Gaelic *tonn a chladaich*, Beach Wave.

Pink are the flamingoes on a travel brochure, pink are the ballet shoes on the cover of a book, pink are the towels in the guest bathroom, pink is the colour of a manicure set.

Pink can be used to soften jagged outlines, providing the rose-coloured glasses which protect one from harsher reality.

Pink is the dressing gown of the late-rising star, pink the pantaloon of the comedy clown, pink the cravat of a man about town.

Pink is the light in an underground bar, pink is the sunset seen from afar. Pink is the cloud one must descend from too soon, pink is the shape just seen in a shower.

To pink is to lightly wound a duelling opponent, to pink is to shear a serrated edge, to pink is to hear an engine unhappy with its fuel.

Western people, it is said, prefer colours in the order: blue, red, green, purple, orange and yellow. Intermediate colours are usually felt to be less pleasant than pure colours. And when it comes to remembering, tests show that although describable shades run into thousands, the ones we are first to recall are: red, pink, orange, yellow, green, blue, purple and brown.

For pink is perfection, and the best of them all.

"From every blush that kindles in thy cheeks,
Ten thousand little loves and graces spring
To revel in the roses."

Nicholas Rowe, *Tamerlane*

"I know not which I love the most,
    Nor which the comeliest shows,
The timid, bashful violet
    Or the royal-hearted rose:

The pansy in her purple dress,
    The pink with cheek of red,
Or the faint, fair heliotrope, who hangs,
    Like a bashful maid her head."

Phebe Cary, *Spring Flowers*

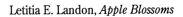

"The apple blossoms' shower of pearl,
    Though blent with rosier hue,
As beautiful as woman's blush
    As evanescent too."

Letitia E. Landon, *Apple Blossoms*

Rhapsody in Blue

Blue is the colour of constancy, of faithfulness, of unchangingness. Blue is the sky, the deep sea, the colour of ice-cold distant stars. Blue is the firmament, the vault of heaven, an eternal canopy above. Blue is for astronauts, and the infinities of space they encounter. Montgomery's armoured legions of the Western desert christened it 'The Blue', the beyond, and thought of it as immeasurable distance.

Blue is for sincerity, the wide-open blue eyes that cannot deny.

Blue are the eyes of the pioneer, seeking ever-distant horizons; blue are the eyes of the hill-shepherd squinting into the early dawn; blue are the eyes of the mariner scouring infinite sea.

Blue is the aristocrat of colours, the blue-bloods who champion the cause, the conservatives who changeth not, the athletes who triumph at ancient universities.

Blue also belongs to the plebeians, chanting 'Up The Blues' as they follow their soccer heroes into battle with those others who are attired in the red-and-white scarves of a continuing enemy.

Blue is the sound of music: the rhythm of percussion, the sad lament of the long-oppressed, the rhapsody of tune, the melody of form, the elegant waltz.

Blue is a changing host of colours, from azure to cobalt, indigo to navy, steel to turquoise. Brunswick blue, Capri blue, Chinese blue, Dresden blue, Persian blue, Prussian blue. Blue is the willow pattern, the Delft tile, the Gobelin tapestry, the Wedgwood saucer.

Blue was the warrior's woad, the sailor's serge, the poilus uniform. Blue is the beret of the peace-keeper, blue the anchor-badge on the coxswain's white shirt, blue the coats of the hospital wounded.

Blue is a peacock-feather in an Ascot hat, a sapphire gleaming on a debutante's finger, an aquamarine pendant on a chaperon's front.

Blue are the heavens above, the unchanging sphere, the empyrean welkin, the celestial universe. It is the blue of Milton's 'clear hyaline, the glassy sea'; Omar Khayyam's 'inverted bowl they call the sky' and Shakespeare's 'majestical roof fretted with golden fire'.

Blue is a constant rhapsody of sea and sky.

"A blossom of returning light,
   An April flower of sun and dew;
The earth and sky, the day and night
   Are melted in her depth of blue!"

Dora Read Goodale, *Blue Violets*

"I met her in the greenest dells,
Where dewdrops pearl the wood bluebells;
The lost breeze kissed her bright blue eye,
The bee kissed and went singing by,
A sunbeam found a passage there,
A gold chain round her neck so fair;
As secret as the wild bee's song
She lay there all the summer long."

John Clare, *Secret Love*

Virginal White

White is the overriding symbol of purity, of untarnished innocence, of stainless chastity. This is manifest most openly in the virgin white of the bridal gown, in the full meaning of a white wedding. White is used constantly by poets to portray that cleanliness, that immaculate virtue, that undefiled state, that unsullied, pristine decency. Lawn is as white as the driven snow, girls' skins as white as the swan's neck, the lily, or the dove sent out from the Ark.

The imagery is made stronger when, as it often is, it is contrasted with the opposite of white, that absence of colour which is black. As Shakespeare says in *Romeo and Juliet:*

"For thou will lie upon the wings of night
Whiter than new snow on a raven's back."

Whiter than white: even the white lies of advertising cannot quite destroy the image. Nor can all the unwelcome associations given to whiteness: the useless burden of the white elephant, the white feather of cowardice, the white flag of surrender, the white lightning of bootleg liquor, the white slave on the road to ruin.

The white knight in shining armour, the white angels from their clouds descending, the white pieces on the chessboard privileged to start first, the white snood of a nun, do much to balance this.

Scottish border legend abounds with knights riding white steeds, with their white hounds running beside them as they rode in pursuit of a lady. And of their ladies, with milk-white hands and similar complexions, who generally managed to turn the tables on the knights and their intended seductions.

White in itself would seem to offer some protection, in that the ladies often offer it as an excuse for not greening their gown and thus exciting a jealous husband, father or brother. The knight accepting a postponement of his pleasure finds himself outwitted at the castle gate, or by encountering said husband, father or brother.

So the ladies held out for white sheets and white garments for bed, before that final surrender of innocence.

"Roses at first were white,
    Till they could not agree,
Whether my Sappho's breast
    Or they more white should be."

Robert Herrick, *Hesperides*

"We are Lilies fair,
    The flower of virgin light;
Nature held us forth, and said,
    Lo! my thoughts of white."

Leigh Hunt, *Songs and Chorus of the Flowers*

"Have you seen but a bright lily grow,
    Before rude hands have touched it?
Have you marked but the fall of the snow
    Before the soil hath smutched it? ...
O so white! O so soft! O so sweet is she!"

Ben Jonson, *Celebration of Chares*

Red is for Danger

Those choosing red are making a statement. It is a bold primary colour, it is there to impress, it can never be a half-hearted selection, a choice made merely from happenstance. Red is at the least refracted end of the spectrum, red is for rubies. Red is for hair, for lips, the fox's ruddy coat. Red is for Empire. Red is Revolution. Red is a banner proclaiming belief. Red marks boundaries, charts routes, defines limits.

Red is the flag flying on firing ranges, red controls the onrushing train; red is the signaller's lamp for the ship come ashore.

Red belongs too to the past. Red were the coats of Wellington's men at Waterloo, the highlanders in the thin square in the Crimea, and the dusty soldiery out on the vast-ranging veldt of South Africa. Red were the scarlet cloaks of cavalrymen, the mess-dress regalia of lancers and yeomen. Red is for the blood that was shed on a thousand battlefields of centuries gone by.

Red is for beef, for the healthy cheeks of meat eaters, the all-weather faces of farmers, the rude physiognomy of peasants.

Red is for the hunters, not the gatherers. Red is the warpaint of the Indian brave, red is the autumn coat of the deer slayer, red the jacket of the master of hounds and the king of hearts.

Red is for wine: the claret of Bordeaux, the burgundy of Beaune, the rioja of Spain, the port of Portugal.

Red are the uniforms of the gnomes on hammering anvils in Santa's grotto, red the suit worn by St Nicholas, bringer of gifts, as he descends among the red roofs and chimneys.

Red are the roses, flowering favourite of ten dynasties of poets. Red is the passion of Carmen, the rape of Lucrece, the revenge of Andronicus.

Red is for warmth, the flicker of camp fires, the friendliness of hearths, the comfort of heated rooms. But also of furnaces, fuelled in stokeholds and subterranean passages, to produce steam and power and movement.

Red is for rhythm, and music which stirs and quickens the heart.

Red is for danger, red is a warning.

"Any color, so long as it's red,
   Is the color that suits me best,
Though I will allow there is much to be said
   For yellow and green and the rest."

Eugene Field, *Red*

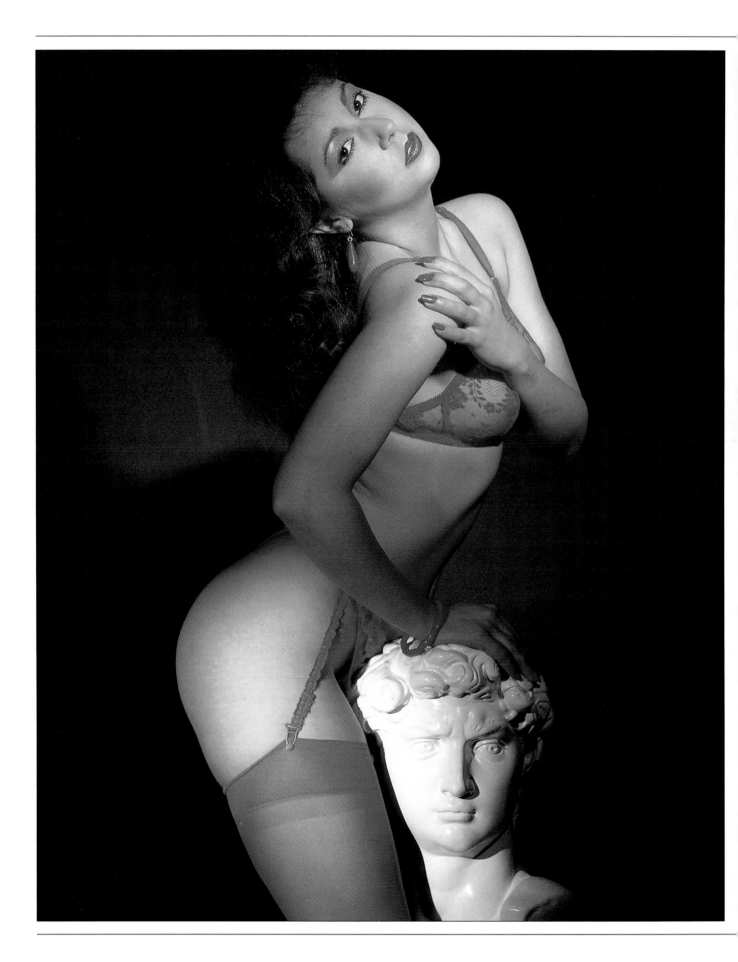

Sensual Lingerie

"Gather ye rosebuds while ye may,
    Old time is still a-flying:
And this same flower that smiles today
    Tomorrow will be dying."

Robert Herrick
To The Virgins, To Make Much Of Time

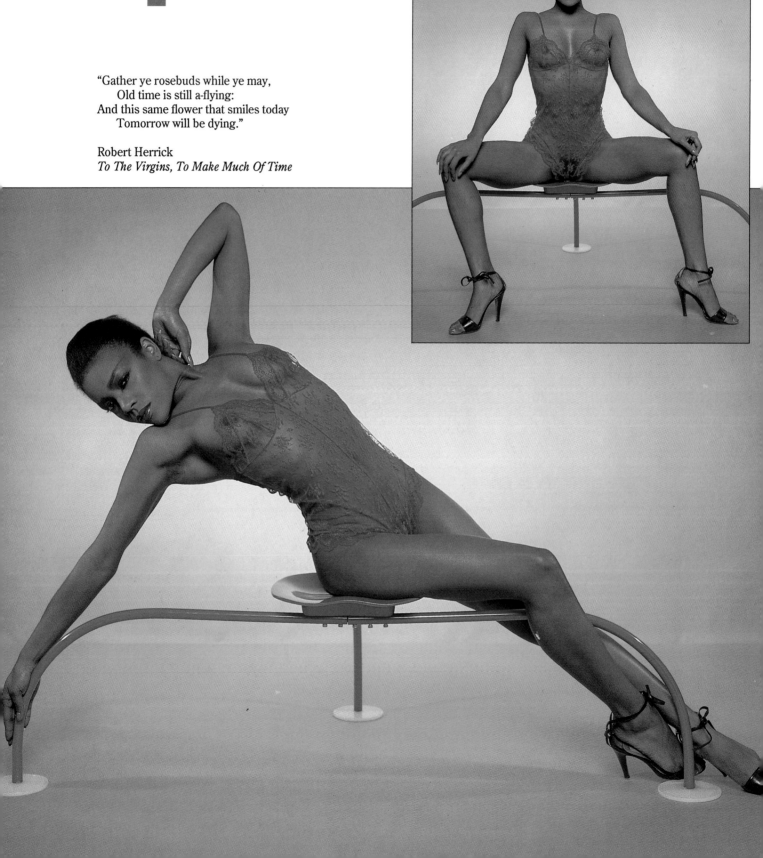

Sensual
Lingerie

Sensual Lingerie

■

Coffee and Cream –
the Perfect Mix

Colour combinations create harmonies or contrasts, from both of which immense pleasure can be derived. Only the artist's or decorator's art can achieve those necessary balances and tones which immediately signal that the mixture is exactly right. Coffee brings to the mix the excitement of Brazil and the rhythms of the Caribbean, the carioca swing of Rio de Janeiro and the steel bands of Trinidad and Tobago.

Coffee is originally of the East, of Abyssinia and Arabia, and derives from that Turkish pronunciation – *kahveh* – of the Arabic *qahwah*, or so the Oxford English Dictionary informs.

The dictionary is less romantic in its definition of cream as the butyraceous part of milk, which gathers on top when the milk is left undisturbed. Only when one carries on to consider the associations and parallels which derive from this emergent superiority does cream begin to sound attractive.

The cream of society, the most excellent element, the quintessence. The best, the nobility, the upper crust, the top people, the elite, the highest, the brass, the *ne plus ultra*, the Establishment.

And the cream derivatives: cream cake, cream tea, cream ware. The luxury of Irish coffee, with cream poured on to the back of a spoon so that it lies on top, concealing the strong spirit below. The creamy foam of Guinness stout, in which one can write one's initials or trace a Valentine's Day heart.

Combine the exotic of coffee and the indulgence of cream and a fresh compound is formed – something superior to its component parts. It is in the coffee-cream combination that the inspiration and stimulation lies. The dark black depths, the rich white creaminess.

Lay one upon the other for greatest effect; each assumes a different character, each brings out something in the other that was not wholly there before. It has become coffee-cream, rather than the coffee and cream it was previously.

Not a primary colour, not a secondary one, but a perfect mixture.

"Good sooth, she is
The queen of curds and cream."

William Shakespeare, *The Passionate Pilgrim*

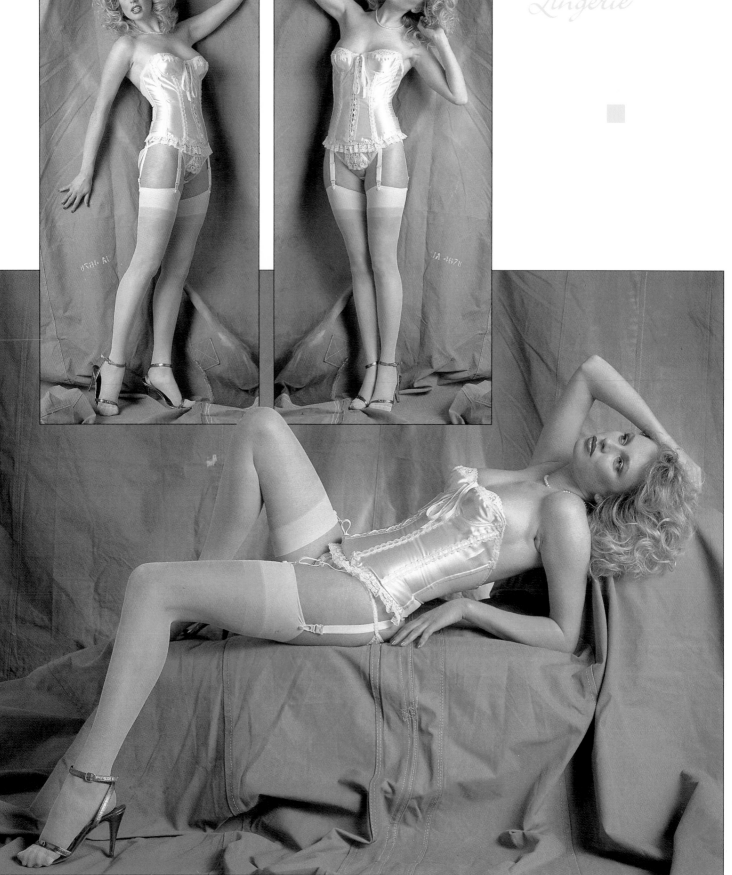

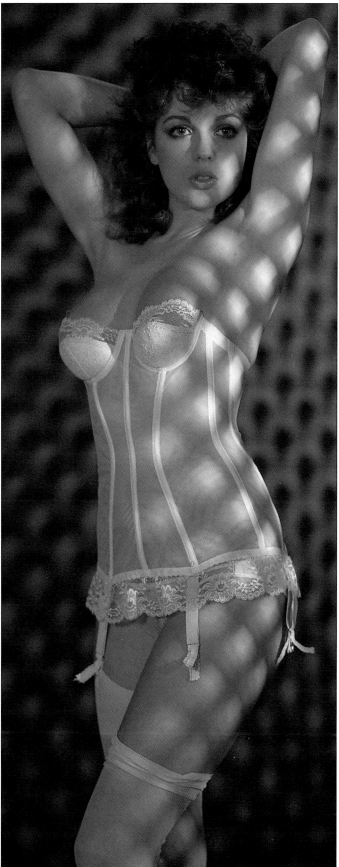

"Come, little cottage girl, you seem
        To want my cup of tea;
And will you take a little cream?
        Now tell the truth to me.

She had a rustic, woodland grin
        Her cheek was soft as silk,
And she replied, Sir, please put in
        A little drop of milk."

Barry Pain, *Wordsworth*

Black Magic

Black is midnight, the bewitching hour, time of the night-people. Black is the eighth colour of the teletext spectrum, the absent colour, the unexpected outline, the colour that exists when all other colours are off the stage, are unlit, are unseen. Black is a symbol of mysteries to come, a signal to be followed, accompanying the moonlit path to explore, the night to be examined, the darkness to be braved and penetrated.

Black are the gowns of the magic-makers: academics and clergymen, Merlins and Mephistopheles. Black is the uniform of the seductress: the flamenco and can-can dancers, the cafe waitresses and the girls in the windows by the canals of Amsterdam.

Black is the colour offered openly to the world by widows, seeming to mourn for what is past without denying that there is a future. Black is the colour of the all-purpose little black dress, to suit the occasion of theatre-dinner or reception, clandestine meeting or stroll in the park, conference or cocktail-hour.

Black is lace, and frills, and the naughtiness of the *Vie Parisienne* of one's youth. Black is forbidden fruit, and darkness at noon.

Black is the colour of temptation, the indulgent box of chocolates consumed on the chaise-longue in the afternoon.

Black are the thunderstorms that loom on the horizon, black are the clouds that scud across the sea, black are the sea-depths into which the diving-bell descends, black are the underground seams of coal.

Black are the omens that the soothsayer foretells, black are the tea-leaves that the fortune-teller reads, black are the signs the wizard has seen, black are the cards dealt out by gypsy hands.

Black are the smuggler's horses running through the night, black are the pit-ponies immured in the mine, black are the chargers of the cavalry's last gallant ride, black is the stallion of the sheikh's rapturous bride.

Black is the magic that all this can survive, black the friendly dark that offers comfort and surprise, black is the oblivion that sleep provides.

Black is night, black is mysterious, black is kind.

"Round her eyes her tresses fell,
Which were blackest none could tell,
But long lashes veiled a light,
That had else been all too bright."

Thomas Hood, *Ruth*

FUJI-RF

19A 19B

"A Persian's Heaven is easily made:
'Tis but black eyes and lemonade."

Thomas Moore, *Intercepted Letters*

"Dear night! this world's defeat;
The stop to busy fools; care's check and curb;
The day of spirits; my soul's calm retreat
Which none disturb."

Henry Vaughan, *The Night*

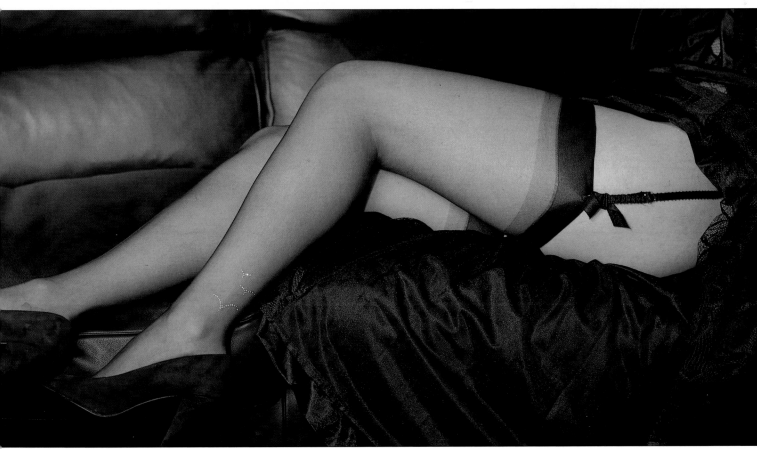

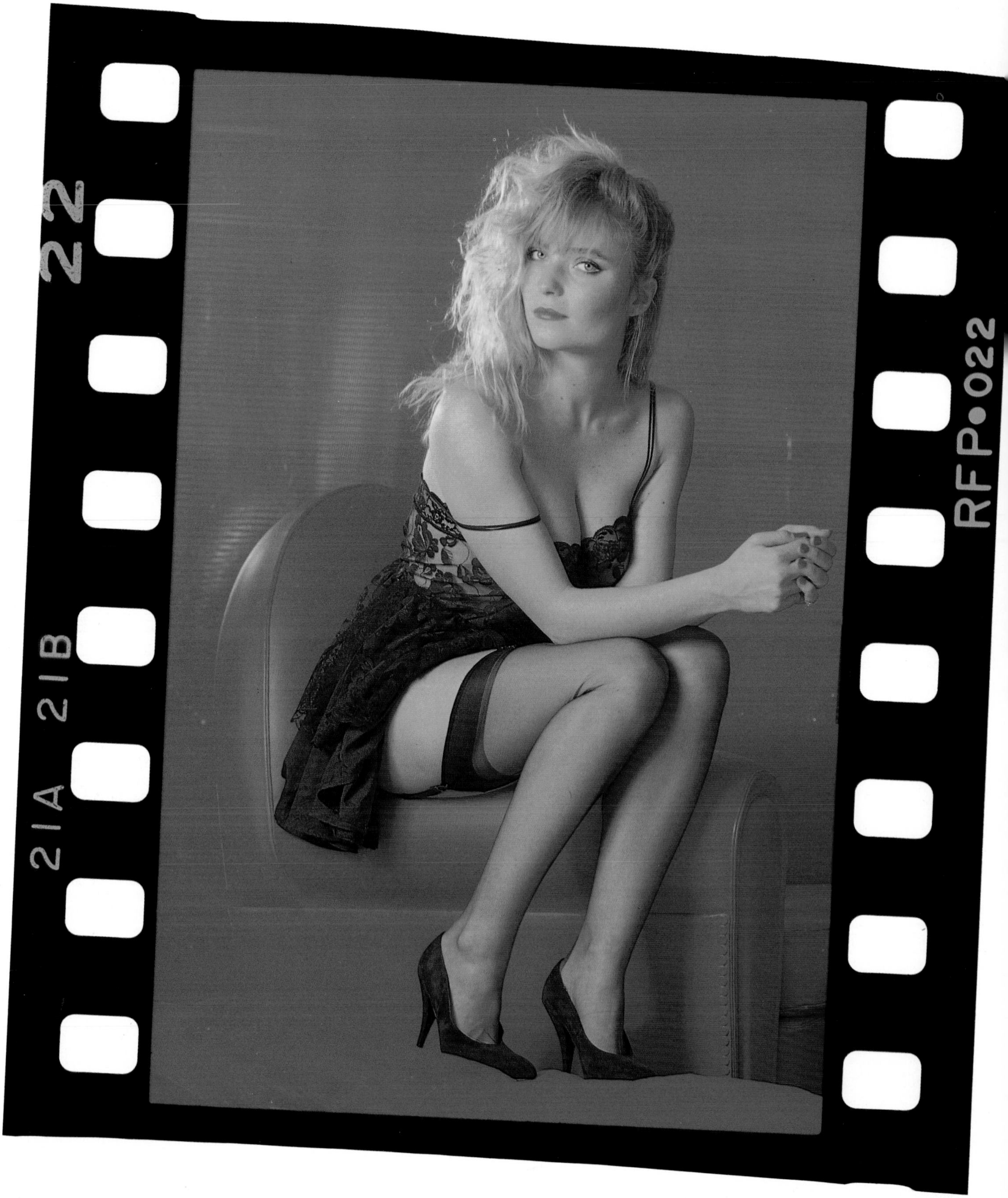
22
21A
21B
RFP•022

"Heaven's ebony vault,
Studded with stars, unutterably bright,
Through which the moon's unclouded grandeur rolls,
Seems like a canopy which love has spread
To curtain her sleeping world."

Percy Bysshe Shelley, *Queen Mab*

Luminescent Lilac

Luminescence is the condition or quality of emitting light other than as a result of incandescence. Lilac seems to have this quality in a way that none of the other colours we have studied seem to do. The very word Lilac itself travelled from afar, coming to English from the French, derived from the Spanish, who took it from their Arab invaders, who probably originally took it from Persia.

Lilac is a strong word with poets, who often associate its colour with the precious stone amethyst. It seems unromantic to analyse amethyst and find it is a quartz, coloured by manganese or by a compound of iron and soda.

Perhaps the best-known reference to lilacs is in T.S. Eliot's magnificent poem *The Waste Land* with its opening:

> "April is the cruellest month, breeding
> Lilacs out of the dead land, mixing
> Memory and desire, stirring
> Dull roots with spring rain."

Lilac suggests a rebirth, a rejuvenescence, a flowering again after the seasonal death of the land in winter.

Pursuing our horticultural detective work, aided in particular by Geoffrey Grigson's excellent book *The Englishman's Flora*, one finds the Lilac-flower is a West Country name for the fragrant Water Mint. Because of its smell, falling halfway between that of the ordinary garden mint and peppermint, this lilac-flowered mint was strewn in medieval days on the tables and floors where banquets were held. In even earlier days it was sacred to Aphrodite, goddess of love.

From there it is perhaps not too great a jump to that most venereal of lilac-coloured flowers, the Early Purple Orchid (*Orchis mascula*). One need not labour the point, but its name stemmed from the Greek for testicle, because of its two root tubers. One of these, a new firm one, stored food for next season; the other, an old slack one, was drawn upon for present needs. Ancient writers said that the Thassalian women produced two goat's milk potions from each of the tubers: one for increasing desire, one for deterring it.

Perhaps this is why poets sing the praises of the lilac-coloured.

"The whole east was flecked
With flashing streaks and shafts of amethyst,
While a light crimson mist
Went up before the mounting luminary,
And all the strips of cloud began to vary
Their hues, and all the zenith seemed to ope
As if to show a cope beyond the cope!"

Epes Sargent, *Sunrise at Sea*

"I remember, I remember
    The roses, red and white,
The violets and the lily-cups,
    Those flowers made of light!
The lilacs where the robin built,
    And where my brother set
The laburnum on his birthday, –
    The tree is living yet."

Thomas Hood, *I Remember, I Remember*